Peace In Hope And Heartache

Leah Ellis

BookLeaf Publishing

India | USA | UK

Made with ❤ on the BookLeaf Publishing Platform
www.bookleafpub.in
www.bookleafpub.com

Dedication

To all those with the pull of potential tugging at their heart, with pain, passion, and hope for tomorrow.

Preface

This collection is my story, my journey. It's about the moments that shape us, the loves that hold us, and the losses that change us. From the quiet, tender spaces of motherhood to the raw ache of grief, these words attempt to capture the complexities of a life lived in all its layers. In the heartache, I've found resilience. In the fleeting beauty of everyday moments, I've found hope.

As you read, you'll feel the pull between sorrow and joy, loss and love. Life isn't linear. It bends, breaks, and blossoms in ways we never expect. There's no perfect version of who we are—just growth, transformation, and the connections that make the journey worth it.

Walk with me through these pages. Reflect on your own story, find solace in shared experiences, and remember: even in the darkest times, there's always a seed of hope waiting to grow.

Acknowledgements

To my husband and my children your love is the quiet rhythm that guides me. You've been my inspiration and my reason to write through every fleeting moment. To my dear friends, you've walked with me through the highs and the lows, offering support and light when I needed it most. Your presence in my life is a gift I cherish more than words can say. In this journey of words and life, you are my home. Thank you for holding me up, for believing, for always being the gentle push that keeps me moving forward.

Metamorphosis

Sometimes, the stages of life
feel like the metamorphosis
from caterpillar to butterfly.
But humans aren't so simple as that.
We don't have a simple flow -
egg, larva, pupa, adult.
We start out small, and that is true.
Tiny babies who rely on love.
And small children counting
on parents to guide them.
But then we reach the transformation
from dependent to independent.
Maybe?
Are we ever really independent?
We grow and change through
each of our life stages.
But never are we all alone.
And we always need each other.
Metamorphosis is a fun thought.
An idea that we can reach a "final stage"
but humans aren't as simple as that.
We grow, and we change
throughout our lives.
Our metamorphosis is never complete.

Embrace the growth and the change
as every day is a new opportunity.

Motherhood

Sometimes, my heart hurts from deep within.
Memories of lives long since lived.
Dreams of days that were once blissful tomorrows
have turned into entries in the book of yesterday.
Motherhood is a constant pull to stop time in its tracks
while fantasizing about what the future will hold.
Every moment is fleeting and unfairly fast
but excitement for what's to come pulls us forward.
Tiny fingers stretch out and suddenly become
Sticky toddler hands reaching out for help washing as
Lotioned preteen hands stand next to me at the sink, but
then the
Manicured hands of a young woman wave goodbye as
she leaves.
Where has the time gone?
This blink-and-you'll-miss-it life is a thief.
I want to hold them a little longer.
Sometimes, my heart aches to know
They will never be this small again.

An Open Letter to My Womb

Oh, Great Grower of Life
Why do you destroy
That which you should nurture?
Oh, Great Grower of Life
What gives you the right
To decide for me?
Oh, Great Grower of Life
I can feel your wretched emptiness
Where I should be filling flips and kicks
Oh, Great Grower of Life
You steal from me
Again and Again
Oh, Great Grower of Life
I hate you
You are not great
You fail more than you succeed
Oh, You empty, ugly thing
Why can't you do your job?

The Moments that Make You

As I check my email, I see the words;
 "We predict Connie is your grandmother."
Seconds later comes the message,
"Hello, Leah."
Suddenly panicked, I can't reply,
and instead, I call my mom.
Overwhelmed, I call my husband
scaring him with my lack of coherent speech.
After a time, a meek "Hello."
back to my new grandma.
Then, more messages.
Her.
Her husband - Grandpa.
He can't wait to meet me.
More time passes -
and many tears are shed.
Soon,
An Aunt,
A cousin
And my dad!
The night is spent connecting.
With them
With the lost part of me.

It is indescribable.
I am welcome.
I am loved.
I no longer have a missing piece.
I'm a different woman today
than I was yesterday.

Untitled

In my living room, two little girls and a cat are napping. Sitting on my cozy gray couch, I can feel a breeze coming in through the open front door. The distant sounds of sirens and bird chirps sneak in, distracting me from the task at hand. On one end of the couch, a tiny blonde lump rests her head on the armrest, body bound in an aqua cocoon of fluff and pom-poms. Some people might call it a throw; she calls it Heaven. Her face reveals the slightest smile indication of good dreams. The blanket drifts slowly up and down as she breathes, but the cat at her feet doesn't seem to mind. The sleek black and white frame of feline royalty nests in the tangle of fuzz, sharing her warmth with the child and enjoying the heat of the blanket beneath her. At the opposite end, I sit with my legs in a knot. There is a distinct weight on my thighs, placed there by yet another sleeping body. Curly strawberry blonde hair is visible as I glance down, her face turned in toward my body. I can hear tiny breaths whispering in and out as her chest rises and falls in a steady rhythm. A spot of warmth and humidity is forming on my left hip, where a face has fallen limp. Beneath the weight of two sleeping girls and a cat is my favorite place to be.

Count

I hold up my fingers as a tiny voice recites,
"one - two - three - four - FIVE!"
Counting with me, he shows off his skills.
"six - seven - eight - nine - TEN!"
The voice of a toddler becoming
the voice of a preschooler.
"Eleven - twelve - fifteen - sixteen - TWENTY."
He's counting with me - showing me what he knows.
He's counting on me - to guide him when he falters.
Counting with him is the easy part.
"Eleven - twelve - thirteen - fourteen - fifteen."
Concrete skills to help him grow.
Teach him counting, letters, shapes, and colors.
Someday, he'll learn division, spelling, geometry, and art.
Guiding him is harder, though.
There is no skill progression chart
on manners, morals, or acting with heart.
There is no easy mode for teaching
justice, liberty, freedom, or compassion.
My little boy will be a man one day.
An advocate for hope.
He's counting on me to guide him now.
I'm counting on him to guide our future.

"The youngest"
"The middle"
"One of the Bigs"
Where do you fall
when your role
keeps changing?
What is your role
when the expectations
keep changing?
The little and the big.
Not the baby.
Not the oldest.
A leader in your own way.
Spirited, stubborn, and free.
The expectations change.
But you don't.
You know who you are
with a passion I envy.
Your role may change.
But you don't.
You hold tight
to being who you are.
You don't follow
if you don't want to.

You stand tall
when you set
your mind to a task.
You may be "the sequel" but you
are never just the second child.
You are the first like you.
Every brilliant bit of you.

Tiny Drummer

Thump, thump, thump, thump,
the steady sound of tiny hands
smacking against a tiny belly.
Thump, thump, thump, thump.
She giggles as she stares
across the room to the face
of the whole world - at least,
in her eyes.
Thump, thump, thump, thump,
the tiny drummer sets her beat
pat, pat, giggle, pat, pat, giggle
Thump, thump, thump, thump.
Mommy's eyes beam
when she sees the show.
She smiles at her baby,
who seems in a hurry to grow.
Thump, thump, thump, thump,
Mama joins the band.
Thwap, thwap, thwap, thwap.
Thump, thump, thump, thump.
The sound of Mom and Daughter
lost in their own world.
One made from belly drums
and giggles from little girls.

A Poem to My Son

Oh, my little Victory.
You are a beast of a boy.
In all the best ways.
You rawr with energy
a kinetic force like none other.
You are clever like a raven,
always keeping me on my toes.
My silly little chimpanzee,
you climb and run and dance.
Brave and kind and loving
you are a gentle, mighty soul.
Oh, you are a beast of a boy.
And I love it so.

Eldest

The first...

...to hear my heart from inside.

...to make me a mother.

...to fill me with pride.

...to inspire my awe.

...to test my patience.

...to see me cry.

...to break my heart.

Sweet girl, sometimes I forget.

All my firsts are your firsts, too.

Eldest daughter to Eldest daughter -

sometimes it feels like a lot.

The pressure to be a role model

and third-in-command.

Not a parent, but parent-adjacent.

The ownership of protecting your siblings.

But, dear daughter, I want you to know

You don't have to hold that burden.

Mom and Dad are here for them.

And we are here for you, too.

You don't have to be the strong one

Or fill yourself with 'responsibility.'

Give yourself a chance to be a kid.

To be a little wild, a little reckless.

You have years to be an adult,
To be the amazing leader
you are so ready to be.
But slow down. Find the whimsy
Find the joy in your world.
The woman you will be
is counting on the girl you are.
Help her learn her lessons
So she can have her turn.

Fleeting

"The days are long,
but the years are short."
A phrase muttered to
every tired toddler mom
by an experienced mother
at one point or another.
"Yeah, right," the tired mom
thinks to herself as she sighs.
The threenager has snatched
another toy from the toddler,
and now they are both screaming.
"The days are long.
The years are long.
The naps are short."
The tired mom writes
in a text to her friend.
The long days continue on.
But the years begin to shorten.
How does time move so fast?
Yesterday, they fought over
"Sofia the First" and "Paw Patrol."
Today, they argue over
who gets to use the computer first.
They have friends to message

and photos to share.
Their little-kid-ness is going away.
"Big Kid" has a whole new meaning.
Tomorrow, they will want to know
who gets to borrow Mom's car.
There will be dances and dates
Shopping trips, movies,
and meals with friends.
Mom will lose her place as
Confidant #1. The years,
my, they sure are short.
But in these long days,
Mom will always be close by.

Christmas Morning

"I'm on the Nice List!"
screeches an excited voice,
waking me from my slumber.
"MOM! DAD! Look at this!"
Little voices call out for us,
Joy and excitement in every breath,
and dripping from every word.
They've waited all year for this morning.
Presents, surprises, and rules ignored.
There is laughing, and sharing,
and candy for breakfast, of course.
After opening boxes and building toys,
we watch them play together.
The memories create themselves,
in front of our very eyes.
This bond of sibling love they share
ebbs and flows as they learn who they are.
They fight as they determine their boundaries,
but they love each other in quiet ways.
Christmas morning is a magical time.
But every day is magical, too.
They are the magic in my life.
And I create the magic for theirs.

Sisters

By blood and by birth
sisters, I have none.
By choice and by love
sisters, I have many.
These sisters, I have claimed,
gathered and collected.
As partners in motherhood,
family, business, and community.
My sisters in life who love
not from requirement but by choice.
Sister, who loved me when I was alone.
And sat with me when I was weak.
Sister, I love you.
Sister, who found me when you were lost.
And invited me to your brightest days.
Sister, I love you.
Sister, who gives selflessly to her community
And allows me to contribute with you.
Sister, I love you.
Sister, who leads with grace and confidence,
And believes that I can lead, too.
Sister, I love you.
Sisters with your daughters strong and brave,
And who lead wild girls with me.

Sisters, I love you.
Sisters I have claimed,
gathered, and collected.
Sisters, I love you.

Community

Friends. Community. Tribe.
Your People.
Those few that do life
parallel to your life.
A network of humanity
on the darkest of your days.
The ones who deliver casseroles
on days of births and deaths.
Friends to celebrate weddings
and the union of love and family.
Those that hold your heart
across miles and oceans.
Our souls crave the nostalgia,
the safety, the peace
of togetherness.
Generations of ancestors
built on connections
to each other
and to Earth.
The very rhythm of nature
is built into our bloodlines.
Our connections are interwoven
into the trees and Oceans.
Like the Earth,

our connection is eternal.
Our lives are intertwined in a tapestry
of history that cannot be undone.
Our community is a piece of our soul.
Our friends. Our Tribe. Our Peace.

Our Tree

This is our tree.
Today, we planted this tree.
We broke the ground
with golden shovels.
And cut a ribbon
with giant scissors.
We buried the roots
And took pictures with smiles.
Today, how we celebrate our tree!
We ooh, and we ahh over our tree.
Tonight, we all go home.
The party is over
And the planting is done.
Our tree will live here.
It will create oxygen
and start to take hold.
Its roots will grow deep.
And its branches will stretch.
Over the years, we will grow.
From elementary school
to middle school, we will go.
Our tree will grow, too.
It will grow tall and its branches wide.
Its leaves will shade us

as we play, sing, and read below.
From middle school to high school
Faster than our parents hope.
Our tree will look over us.
It will grow over our city.
Its branches will house birds,
And bugs, and so many creatures.
When we are adults, our tree will still be here.
Children will play under its shade
and enjoy the sounds of its leaves in the wind.
Today, we planted this tree.
Forever, we will celebrate our tree.

Lego

"Love" is a four-letter word.
Filled with meaning and emotion.
To love someone is to give of yourself
your time, your energy, and your future.
You fill your heart with hope for them.
My love for my children
dreams of their futures.
Their lives, their triumphs,
and their adventures.
My love for my husband
holds his hand as he drives.
It has aged to a silent
and ever-present
beating of my heart
and his - together.
Love in a home with four kids
can feel rushed and overlooked.
Connections can be missing
in the rush of diaper changing
and event planning.
But today, love is spoken
in a different four-letter word.
Love looks a lot like "Lego"
Hers built before his.

Time that is given as a gift.
Creating something beautiful
to remind her that he loves her
with something as small as a
Lego.

Delicates

Wash me on the "delicate" cycle.
My soul is feeling thin.
I'm made of lace and chiffon.
The agitation might undo me.
I'm tired deep within my pores.
My cup has nothing left to pour.
I fight to create the peace they need.
These days, I don't know how to proceed.
I fight to create peace.
But when will I feel a piece?
I'm desperate to project hope
though some days it feels out of scope.
Wash me on the "delicate" cycle.
My soul is feeling thin.
I'm made of lace and chiffon.
The agitation might undo me.
Ask me what I live for -
I would give anything for these four.
The future makes me nervous,
but I know we can be of service.
Wash me on the "delicate" cycle.
My soul is feeling thin.
I'm made of lace and chiffon.
The agitation might undo me.

I will lead my merry band
so we can love and protect the banned.
The future is in their hands
and I know where our family stands.

Loss

There is a pain unlike any I have known.
An ache in my soul that I am sure will never fade.
It haunts me at all hours and makes me question myself.
Grief comes in tidal waves sometimes.
Your name on old memories crushes me in its depth.
I flashback to the moment you were torn from my life,
the words echoing from the phone.
Questions that will never be answered
and problems that can never be solved.
The loss of a friend so dear
he was called Brother,
and then he was gone.
Somedays, the grief is a drip from a faucet.
Small but consistent.
Moments where you're missing
in the rhythm of routine.
A reminder that you
are no longer a phone call away.
The pain of your memory breaks my heart,
but seeing the heartbreak in my children is worse.
An uncle stolen from them,
and his playfulness sorely missed.
Our family was shattered
and sometimes I wonder

how we will ever be whole.
I always look for a resolution,
but in this, there is no answer.
The ending simply is.

An Anchor

Is it a gift
or a curse
to be the anchor
of someone's life?
"Feet anchored to the floor."
Unable to move.
"Anchoring her as she sobs."
Supported and cared for.
"Anchored in the chaos."
Held fast - or trapped?
If I am
the anchor
in your life,
am I the prison
or am I
the light post?

Peace, Music, Sight, and Victory

Once upon a time,
the fairy tales always start,
but sometimes, the princess
begins in conflict.
There is no steady building
of first a rising action.
The plot skips straight to the climax.
Intensity is high and the stakes are higher.
This is how her story began.
But then a twist is thrown our way.
Peace, Music, and Sight
join their brother Victory.
A Gift from God has brought them here
to turn the chaos into hope.
The broken princess finds her crown.
A mission, purpose, and desire
to grow and watch them grow, too.
Her once upon a time was dark,
a story she thought had broken her heart.
But the story kept progressing.
And the magic in her world is all from her.
Made with a Gift from God
And called Peace, Music, Sight, and Victory.

Word of the Year

Ah, December is coming to an end.
Talk of resolutions, goals, and visions
are becoming the norm of the day.
Who will you be in the year to come?
How will you change to be more next year?
What is your Word of the Year?
What is your resolution?
What if, this year, I have no resolve?
Or what if I resolve to just be me?
What if I don't subscribe to this belief
that the calendar changes so I must, too?
The new year will be here soon.
And in it I resolve to skip the resolutions.
I resolve to love myself as I am.
To love my life, my kids, and my home.
I resolve to be more of me
and less of what the world wants me to be.
If you ask for my word of the year.
My answer will be
Peace.